T0143988

HIGH SCHOOL SPORTS UNITES A COMMUNITY

Written by
JAMES ANDERSON

AuthorHouse™
1663 Liberty Drive
Bloomington, IN 47403
www.authorhouse.com
Phone: 833-262-8899

This book is printed on acid-free paper.

ISBN: 978-1-6655-4109-1 (sc)
ISBN: 978-1-6655-4108-4 (e)

Print information available on the last page.

Published by AuthorHouse 10/18/2021

authorHOUSE®

Contents

INTRODUCTION

One of the great benefits of high school sports is how it can unify a community who is in support of its youth by attending games, and cheering the team on to victory. Such was the case for the Oakwood Academy Stingers of 2021. The Stingers had created a reputation of excellence under the leadership of their head man The Skipper Fred Apt and his right hand man Assistant Chris Dutton, who is called affectionately "Duttie" by his friends at his request. Brilie Walker and Makenzie Buzzell also coach the Stingers.

THE START OF THE SEASON

There had been a world wide pandemic that took many lives. Everyone was wearing face masks and keeping a social distance of six feet. The community had to spend a great deal of time in quarantine. Football season had to be cancelled, and winter sports was played without fans in the stands. With vaccinations to the disease everyone was anxious for spring sports to begin. As is the case in Maine, outdoor weather in the spring is slow to arrive. Therefore the Baseball and Softball teams began practice indoors. Oakwood Academy has a beautiful indoor facility with a batting cage and room for pitchers and catchers to throw and catch. The softball team had played excellent ball the year previous but they were hurt by graduation. None the less, The Skipper had a great track record of player development. The team had been hurt by the pandemic the previous year when the season had to be shut down early at the Principles Association's request. Coaches did not know how to piece together line-ups until they could get out on the field in the spring. Of course every team in Maine was in the same pickle until the snow melted off the fields. Early season game victories would figure in large when it came to end of the season playoffs.

STINGERS ROSTER

PITCHER...Ring My Bell
CATCHER...Carrie "Nails" Barry
FIRST BASE..Josie Wales
SECOND BASE...Judy JJ Johnson
THIRD BASE..Betsy Walker

SHORT STOP..Ruby Beans
RIGHT FIELD...Kimberly Johnson
CENTER FIELD..Andrea Watson
LEFT FIELD...Debbie Sanders
UTILITY... Wendy Peppercorn

THE STINGERS BEGIN THEIR SEASON ON THE ROAD

In anticipation of a new season the Stingers opener would be postponed due to snow. Everyone would have to wait a week for the opener. Unfortunately, the snow meant the practice field would not be ready until the snow melted.

FINALLY THE STINGERS START THEIR SEASON AT BIRCHWOOD

The time had finally come for the season to begin. The Stingers traveled to Birchwood to play one week late. No one knew what to expect; only that Birchwood had a strong reputation of excellence in the past. Pitcher Ring My Bell was anxious to begin the season and dominated the game. In the circle Ring My was right on the corners with her pitches. She got ahead of hitters on her way to striking out 17 Birches. This limited Birchwood in their attempt to score. In fact Ring My's control limited the Birches to only one runner reaching as far as third. Meanwhile, the Stingers bats remained silent as well. That is until the sixth inning when Judy Johnson walked, followed by a Kimberly Johnson walk bringing up up Ring My with a chance to knock in two with a base hit. With two outs and a two ball two strike count the Birches pitcher went for the strikeout with a high and outside riseball. But the left-handed Bell was ready for this pitch. Ring My lined a sharp hit right down the left field foul line. It would be a triple, with the two baserunners scoring easily on the hit. The Skipper had been encouraging his players to go to the opposite field on the outside pitch and that was just the advice that provided the game winning hit. In looking back, it was a pitchers mistake to try throwing a high outside pitch past Ring My Bell. It had as much of a chance of working as a farmer trying to slip sunrise past his best rooster. It was a 2-0 win for the Stingers thanks to their Senior pitcher. The Stingers had their cross town rival Maplewood up next at home where the home town crowd would get their first look at this years edition of the Oakwood Softball nine. The team would then travel to Maplewood the following week to complete the home and home mini-series.

STINGERS HOST MAPLEWOOD

The Maplewood Monks came to Oakwood off an opening game loss to the Pine Tree Cones. This early in the season however it was hard to tell if one team had the edge over the other, so the Oakwood skipper pumped up the fact that the Maplewood team was a neighboring town rival, and this was a bragging rights game. It worked as the Stingers would win once again by a 2-0 final. The importance of this win would not be known until the regular season ended. One thing would become known, which was that the community would be at home games in support of the Oakwood team. The look at the field was a different look because of the pandemic. No one would be allowed to spectate from behind the chain-link fence, around home plate, and everyone must wear a mask. The parents, grandparents, and locals would settle behind the home run fence beyond left field. Opponents fans would be directed to the same space beyond the right field home run barrier. Every home game fans seemed to return to the same spots for spectating. You could see the field from your car from behind the chain link fence in both left and right field. Some fans chose to watch from their cars. Especially if it was cold, or buggy. After all it was black fly season in Maine. It was a good deal for handicapped folks or the elderly.

At the Maplewood game Ring My stepped into the circle with confidence once again striking out 13 batters with 0 hits, while walking 0. The Stingers bats were silent except for catcher "Nails Barry who with one swing of the bat accounted for the Stingers two runs. The Skipper was not surprised by the lack of hitting, because hitting against live pitching which would allow for instruction and added experience, was not possible until the Stingers could practice outside. "Nails's" home run in the bottom of the fifth was a total surprise. "Nails" was an athlete who just had a way of figuring things out. She had hit the ball hard to left but her first home run was much more of a power blast. She caught on to working the count in her favor, then looked for the meatball, because the pitcher had to throw a strike. The Skipper loved coaching "Nails"because she listened and internalized his information. Her home run traveled right into the rooters section of the home town crowd. Nails's father in fact retrieved the ball, and was saving it to give to her at home that night. After the game the Stingers would begin looking forward to the rematch at Maplewood the following Wednesday.

REMATCH AT MAPLEWOOD

The following Wednesday would come quickly and with the game the Skipper decided to change the hitting philosophy from "up the middle" to just get the ball in play. Force the opposition to make a play. The girls looked much more relaxed in the batter's box. The hits would come, the coaches believed. The offense in the rematch would be provided by "Nails." Carrie would blast her second home run in two games in the seventh which complimented another magnificent pitching performance by Ring My Bell, who struck out 15 while walking 0. The 1-0 win was the Stingers third in a row. The following week would have two very tough games that had to be postponed and rescheduled. This would provide some much needed outdoor practice time. With the game experience that was lost. The Skipper asked the AD if she would schedule a friendly(a practice game where coaches can stop play for learning instruction).

It would be a turning point in the season. The friendly would be with cross state rival Torrence Torpedoes. The Torpedoes needed a friendly for the same reasons. Before the friendly the Torrence coach told the Skipper "score as often as you like because I have some parents who think this Torpedoes team is good.

THE FRIENDLY WITH TORRENCE

The Skipper had hoped the Torpedoes pitcher would challenge Stinger hitters, but she was young and just trying to throw strikes. The Stingers would win easily, behind their Senior pitcher. One thing that would surface was the Oakwood team had trouble scoring from third with no outs. The Skipper would work on a delayed pickle steal. This is where a runner is on first and third. The runner on first would get into a pickle and the runner on third would head home when she thought she could beat the throw in an attempt to score. The final score of the friendly was Oakwood 9 and Torrence 3. As a non league contest the game would not effect the standings in Western Maine class B.

THE STINGERS RETURN TO LEAGUE PLAY

There were make-up games on the schedule. The first one would be a doubleheader against Pine Tree Academy. Ring My Bell would be the starter in the first game, and Oakwood would win by a final of 3-0 score. The big hit offensively for the Stingers was a bit of a surprise as centerfielder Andrea Watson pleasantly surprised the hometown crowd with a bomb to centerfield in the third. Ring My shut down the Cones, and the Oakwood nine took the first game, and was looking for the sweep in game two. The skipper made a change in the circle. He wisely wanted to give his number 2 starting pitcher a chance to pitch. Just in case something happened and Ring My, and she could not pitch down the stretch. No mistake, the skipper realized how fortunate the team was to have RingMy pitch so well in the early season. The move meant Ruby Beans known as "Beanie" would pitch, and Kim Johnson would play short stop. Well Beanie had some trouble finding the strike zone, and that combined with the Cones pitcher Maybel Homes smacking a two run homer in the visitors half of the sixth. Led to a 3-0 loss. Offensively "Beanie" did have one blast into the left centerfield gap in which she got on top of the ball, and ripped it. Unfortunately the Stingers had no baserunners on base, and remained scoreless. The bats would have to come to life if the Oakwood softball nine was to make a run at the state title. On the day the teams would split the doubleheader which kept the capacity crowd grumbling. The players would start a tradition on the afternoon, as after each game they would jog as a group out to the left field fence to thank their supporters for cheering them on. After high fives, and an occasional hug between parent and player. This would be followed by a final word from the coaches.

The final game of the regular season was a loss to division A Boon Town. The loss would not have an effect on the standings, and the skipper would use the loss as a reminder that you must be at your best, every game or desired results may not happen. The good news was the bats began to wake up in the game. JJ got a couple hits, although she was cut down trying to stretch a single into a double. As she jogged off the field the skipper who she so wanted to please called out to her nice hit kid. Always positive that is how the skipper rolled. After the game he would remind JJ that she could swipe second on the catcher all day long, and in this case patience might be a better choice. It's all about preparation. The Stingers would find out they would need to play one more home game, because of the closeness of the standings. Maplewood would come to Oakwood for one more game that would have a direct effect on the standings.

RING MY IS HOSPITALIZED

At Monday's practice Ring My Bell would have trouble breathing so the skip called for an ambulance. She would not be able to play until she could complete a practice. Beanie would be in the circle for Oakwood against Maplewood.

OAKWOOD DEFEATS MAPLEWOOD

Catcher "Nails "Barry had determined that Beanie was too careful in the loss to Pine Tree. She was afraid to throw a ball, and therefore although she had good velocity her pitches were right in the middle of the plate. Ithis game they planned to stay on the corners even if it meant giving up a few walks. The plan worked as Oakwood played solid defense. In the third with Josie Wales on second after a bunt single and a swipe of second Kim Johnson, who was starting to find her groove at the plate, line drove a single to left knocking in the first run of the game. Beanie would adjust her launch angle on her swing matching power with swing angle for a home run to straight away centerfield. Oakwood would win the game 2-0. This coupled with a Pine Tree loss, meant Oakwood would go into the state tournament ranked #1 in the region, and home field until the quarter finals.

FIRST PLAYOFF GAME HOME
VS. BIRCHWOOD

It was time for the first playoff game, and Oakwood would draw #8 Birchwood, who after their opening game loss to Oakwood had gotten on track, and had a good season. Before the game the Parents, Grandparents and fans were all in place when a buzz began to ripple through the crowd. The Oakwood pitcher Ring My Bell had practiced the day before, and would be the starting pitcher for Oakwood. Beanie would return to short stop, and the only unknown was how long Ring My could last. The first pitch was a called strike on the outside corner which seemed to settle the nerves of the Oakwood crowd. Ring My then threw a fastball that was fouled off. The Birchwood batter then swung through strike three, and all seemed well in Stinger nation. The teams would remain scoreless through 4 innings, This added to the stress of the playoff atmosphere. The team to score the first run it felt would have a big advantage. In the top of the fifth Birchwood would get a runner on first on a hit-by-pitch. The Birchwood fans applauded, while the Oakwood fans felt a tightening in their throats. With the Stingers guarding against the bunt, the next batter for Birchwood was a three sport star known very well to the Oakwood fans. Her name was Jansen. With Jansen at the plate the Birchwood coach had no thoughts of a sacrifice bunt. He wanted more. With a 3 ball no strike count Jansen lifted a long deep fly down the right field line towards Kimberly Johnson. From the Oakwood dugout Duttie could only think of the hundreds of flyballs he had hit to Kim during practice sessions. Kim had to go back and towards the foul line to make a play on the ball. The Maplewood fans clapped and cheered as the ball flew. That ray of optimism however was dimmed when Kimberly reached out and cradled the foul fly into her mitt, and quickly returned the ball to the second base bag, followed by an Oakwood cheering round of applause. Those sitting in their cars honked their horns, and Duttie's mom rang her cow bell. The next hitter lined a rocket up the middle where Judy Johnson dove horizontal to the ground for the catch. She scrambled quickly to her feet and made a snap throw to first base to double off the Birchwood runner. The Oakwood fans cheered, and the horns tooted, and of course there was a little cow bell mixed in. The first run was still up for grabs.

THE STINGERS FINALLY SCORE

In the bottom of the inning Oakwood would get a ground ball single to centerfield by Josie Wales, followed by back to back doubles and a 2-0 lead for the Stingers. First it was "Nails" Barry who doubled to left scoring Josie. With a run on the board it seemed the entire stadium exhaled, and the tension broke as Kimberly Johnson stepped into the box as the next Stingers hitter. Kimberly had become a fan favorite as her level of play had lifted as of late. She promptly doubled to knock in "Nails" with an insurance run. After a scoreless inning Birchwood would come up in the top of the seventh with one last chance to catch Oakwood. With the Birchwood coach encouraging his team for one final push the Birchwood bus driver went to the bus, which was parked in the lot just past the right field barrier. The stadium was stone quiet as everyone heard the bus start. Obviously the bus driver wasn't confident of a Birchwood comeback. The Oakwood fans had to chuckle. Then as the stadium settled down and play resumed the bus driver put the bus in reverse causing the warning bell to sound. Once again the Oakwood fans got a chuckle. Shortly there after Ring My would pitch a perfect inning ending the game with Oakwood on top 2-0. The third playoff game would be on Saturday at 11:30. Opponent TBD. The Oakwood fans would go home happy, looking forward to Saturday when they would reassemble.

THE STADIUM FILLS UP

Maybe it was because it was Saturday AM., but the Oakwood fans came out in droves to cheer on their Stingers. Teakwood Academy had a good number of fans as well. Both teams and their fans had a love fest going. You could feel the tension in the air as the two teams jockeyed back and forth for that first run. First Teakwood loaded the bases in the third, with no outs. Then with the bases full a Teakwood batter hit a line drive to right, which Kim Johnson looking into a tough sun sky would lay out flat for the catch. She hopped up quickly to her feet, and seeing the runner off the second base bag she quickly fired to second for the double play. The umpire called out, then spun to see where the runner on third was. She was just half way down the line towards home. Although she would finish, and cross the plate. The umpires would huddle, and determine the runner on third did not score before the third out of the inning, therefore the run would not count. Right or wrong the teams switched sides, New to this years crowd, but well known to the Stinger fan base Sue and J.D. Hill were in attendance. Their two daughters Hannah and Dani had played for the first Oakwood State championship. Hannah was the pitcher, while Dani played 3rd base, and thanks to Johnson's stella play the game remained scoreless. It would stay that way until the bottom of the sixth when the Stingers short stop would come to the plate. She seemed red hot with her new swing angle. But first it would be unfair not to mention that Hannah's catcher on the state championship team was at the game, with her newborn. Yes after a fine college career as a second baseman for The University of Southern Maine Cereise Humphrey would return to Oakwood and fall in love with another Oakwood graduate, the skippers son Fredrick Apt Jr. who was affectionately called "Bo." As Cereise moved from person to person she would say you want to see Little "Bo"? Of course everyone did. He was one of us Oakwoodites. We were all so happy for Cereise, and "Bo." It is almost magical when a community falls in love with the athletes on a high school sports team.

It was time for "Beanie to put an end to this game and send the Stingers to the Quarterfinals of the Region. Ruby Beans stepped up to the plate, and with her new swing angle and lifted one high and deep, but foul. Then with the count now full "Beanie" sent one high, far and gone for the win, Next was #2 Pine Tree Academy the following Wednesday at St. Joe's. The team ran out to left to thank their fans. Amidst honking horns, and a little cow bell then the stadium emptied.

THE REGIONAL AT ST. JOE'S

The Regional final would be played the following Wednesday at 3:30. It would match the #1 Oakwood Stingers vs. The #2 Pine Tree Cones. The Skipper of the Stingers was optimistic especially with the way the Stingers were hitting in the second half of the season. In fact he felt the middle of his line-up of Carrie "Nails Barry, Andrea Watson, and Kimberly Johnson, Now just referred to as the "Whammer" were the best middle order in state history. One of the things coach emphasized I was to be optimistic, and believe in your ability. Another as to be respectful of everyone, and everywhere you might find yourself. That included team mates, Coaches, Umpires, Opponents, teachers, and parents. Once a player said, on the on deck circle oh great two outs, that means I will make the third out. Well in post game the skipper made sure everyone knew that it was not ok to go into the batters box with that thought, and to adjust your self talk, to ok this pitcher can't get me out, because I am too good a hitter. He sometimes had his players practice positive self talk in practice. The community showed up to support their beloved softball girls. Although they had to pay to get into the venue. And seating was spread from the bleachers behind home plate to the hillside down the third base line. The fans seemed to gravitate into their usual comfortable pods.

The game would start out harmlessly, with a foul pop that was caught by :Nails: behind the plate. After a strike out the Cones put together 4 strait hits and scored 2 runs before JJ squeezed the third out on a pop-up. Ok. The skipper said to his team, time to answer. The Stingers recorded two quick outs as Carrie :Nails Barry strode to the plate with two gone. What happened next will forever be fixed in the minds of Oakwood fans memories. :Nails: took two called strikes, then three balls. "Nails" would later say she wanted to make the Cones pitcher work, while timing her pitches. Then with the count full Carrie wiggled her body into a comfortable power stance, On the next pitch "bam" she lifted a fly ball to right, It was high, it was far, and it was over the wall. A newspaper reporter got a snap of the Cones right fielder pressed up against the fence with the ball visibly in Of course Duttie's mom added a little cow bell from up on the hill down the third base line. The photo was in the next days newspaper. It was the answer the skipper had asked for. After that gutsy blast by the Stingers catcher.

The game would settle into a pitchers duel, until the 6th when the Cones would plate another for a 3-1 lead. The skipper was pleased to have kept the Conrs from scoring and increasing their lead while the game was slipping away. In the bottom of the sixth the Stingers needed a rally. Kimberly Jonson would lead off. When the umpire asked for a batter the skipper called her over for one final word. He told her you have worked so hard on your hittingit's now that it will pay off. When the stadium announcer announced Kimberly's name the Oakwood faithful applauded and cheered. As Kim stepped into the left handed batter's box the skipper called out here we go Whammer it's your time kid. With that the Whammer tomahawked a line drive down the first base line. Kim thought about trying for two, but when she tried to shift gears she fell down. She scrambled to her feet and returned to first safely. It was just what was needed. The skipper could not explain it, but he knew it when he saw it. The Whammer loved pressure situations. She once told the skipper pressure makes me feel alive. Feeling pressure is a privilege. The Whammer had a way of transferring any pressure she felt back on the pitcher. Maybe it was the way she confidently strode to the plate. Maybe it was her practice swings, or the way she spit then hit her spit with her bat cutting it in half. She chewed sunflower seeds and maybe it was the way she cracked open the shells allowing the sweet tasting seed fall on to her tongue before spitting out the shells. Maybe it was the fact that she could just flat out hit. Anyway it was a unique talent, and it could swing the game in her teams favor. She was a winner. The hit seemed to upset the Pine Tree pitcher because she suddenly could not throw a strike. She walked the next two batters moving the Whammer to third. Beanie was at the plate banking on a first pitch fastball, which she got Beanie hit the top of the ball propelling it into centerfield knocking in two, and a 4-3 lead for the Stingers. All the Oakwood team needed was 3outs in the bottom of the sixth, and they would play for a state title on Saturday. The lead off hitter for the Cones hit a line drive to the left center gap that Andrea Watson dove for, but came up empty. Pine Tree would score two in the inning, and lead 5-3. Now it was the Cones turn to get 3 outs, and victory, which they did for the win. The Stingers, and their fans who loved them would feel the pangs of defeat, and elimination from the tournament. They would not go to states this season. No more practice, no more bus rides, no more cow bell. On Saturday the Cones would win the state Championship in Brewer. No one from Oakwood would attend.

AWARDS NIGHT

It is a tradition at Oakwood to hold an open to the community awards night to pay tribute to their sports teams. Coaches give out MVP awards and coaches awards, as well as an opportunity for coaches to address their fans and players one final time. It was the skipper's favorite night of the season.

When the skipper was announced to come to the podium he was all smiles.

First of all I would like to thank the players and community for their effort and support this entire season. It sure is fun when you win. I must say however we do not emphasize winning. We believe it is much more important to emphasize what produces wins, and the wins take care of themselves.

EFFORT AND RESPECT

We believe that our players must put in the effort necessary to learn and execute the fundamental's necessary to be respectful to the many complexities of the game of softball. That is a big ask of high school age children. We believe the best way to teach respect is to create a fun and relaxed environment in which we can be our best. We want our players to look forward to every practice and game as well as to learn from each experience we share. Our supporters are a big part of reaching this goal. So we thank our supporters for being so loyal and supportive. A big round of applause from the community followed these words. We also encourage our players to be respectful of everyone. This includes self. team mates, coaches, umpires, parents and fans. We hope those who watch us play recognize this respect when they see it. We think this way of thinking will have lifetime benefits to our players. We teach the game which includes critical thinking while playing. We compliment frequently, and we provide time for working on specific components of the game. If a hitter wants extra hitting practice we stay after practice and provide extra hitting practice setting up game like conditions to practice within. We believe that will translate into successful game experiences. Extra positional practice is available upon request. I can't imagine an accurate count of how many ground or fly balls Duttie has hit after practice. We practice with runners on base to up the intensity of the session. We believe it will translate into successful game play. We want our players to think oh yes I got this. Moving forward with each experience. If they fail we teach "no worries," we got this.

MVP AWARD

How do you pick a MVP from this group of athletes who all grew and matured throughout the season, so I have two. Ring My Bell is one for the way she pitched without fear, and led us through the early season games, and then coming back from a stay in the hospital, and returning to the circle for our playoff run. My other choice is Carrie "Nails" Barry, who came up with the important play all season long. "Nails" loved winning, and she played to win in games, and in practice. The home run she hit in the Regional was the gutsiest at bat I have ever seen. "Nails would work on a suggestion, and put it into game use quickly. As a team within a team "Nails" held the responsibility of lead by example, and that was worth more than one win, and she knew she was doing it, but no matter, what the situation she always came through with whatever was needed. I sure would not want to play against her.

COACHES AWARD

The coaches award is equally hard to choose, but I am pleased to honor the Whammer with this award. Kimberly Johnson became known as the Whammer about mid-season when she worked her way into the hearts of anyone who played or watched this team play. In the first half of the season I put in a designated hitter for the Whammer. When I did that the Whammer looked at me and said, "Challenge accepted". From that point forward the coaches were after practice every time we had practice, and this natural athlete practiced her hitting with fastball after fastball. She became one of our most skilled hitters, as well as, a dependable right fielder. In the last inning of the Regional final the Whammer was up first. I thought about a pinch hitter, when my voice of reason Chris Dutton told me why would you do that, Whammer's the best. I saw that he was right, and then Whammer, as I am sure you all remember hit that wicked shot down the first base line. She would fall down between the first snd second base bags, before she scampered back to first. When I asked her after the game what happened the Whammer told me, "I tricked myself," I should have known. Yes there's nothing like the Whammer. The crowd laughed, then applauded the selection of the Whammer as coaches award recipient. The Skipper would finish with appreciation to all, and an annpuncement that both he and Duttie were retiring as of this second so they could internalize what they all had heard. It was the end of an era. The reporters took photos, and everyone went home. The next time the skipper would have this feeling of joy, would be as a fan.

CARRIE "NAIS" BARRY WINS MISS MAINE SOFTBALL AWARD

At the end of each season the coaches gather to select a miss Maine Softball award. The Oakwood skipper attended to advocate for one of his players. He had gone to the meeting one time before with a player he felt was deserving. That was Hannah Hill, and she was named Miss Maine before leaving that Fall on a full scholarship to Seton Hall, before finishing her college career at U. Maine. This year it was Nails who the skipper believed should be Miss Maine. Skip had the respect of his fellow coaches, so when he spoke others listened. He spoke of how Nails led her team, by example and maturity. He mentioned the home run at the Regional, and how Nails told him that pressure was a privilege. He explained how Nails grit and determination had caught the favor of the Oakwood community of fans. He explained how the team followed her lead, and she never let them down. In the end skip challenged the other coaches to vote for Nails because if there was one player they would love to coach it would be Nails. The skipper came home after that meeting proud to inform the Oakwood community that Miss Maine was an Oakwood Stingers player. It was the final feather in the cap. Of a great high school player.

OAKWOOD WINS SPORTSMANSHIP TEAM AWARD

One more award would come from the meeting. The Principles would honor Oakwood with the team sportsmanship award. It was what the coaching staff had encouraged all season. In good times, and through the rough patches. The community loved this award, and made a banner to hang in the field house. Briley Walker and Makenzie Buzzell would take over the coaching duties the following season, and the Stingers would continue to win, and the community would continue to turnout at games. It was felt by the AD, that the program since things were going well that the positions should be filled from within.

FINAL THOUGHTS FROM THE SKIPPER

With that the skipper tanked the community for their support, and the team for their effort, and let everyone know that without his assistant coaches none of this would have been possible. The players then stood and gave the fans, coaches, and themselves one more round of applause. It was a fitting way to end the evening and the season. It is a unique experience being a participant on a high school sports team. It is special when a community of people get behind their youth and watch faithfully as they play and learn the game. During their season. Falling in love with their effort and improvement, and yes their failures, because when you love you are quick to forget any short comings. Second chances are always available.

When a community gets emotionally involved with the effort of a high school sports team it is like a successful marriage. There is love. Very few high school athletes go on to play college ball. It is very time consuming. You have to have a true passion for the game to play in college. Carrie would play one year of softball at division 3 USM. She continued to hit the ball well, however the coaching focused more on winning than she liked, and there weren't as many fans at the games. She would play for 2 years in college, then give up the game she loved because she never felt the love from the game she had felt playing high school ball for her community. She would find an adult league in the summer, and the relaxed atmosphere made the game enjoyable once more.

I hope you enjoyed this read and don't overlook the fun of following high school sports teams.

BRILIE WALKER NAMED SKIPPER
MAKENZIE BUZZELL TO BE TOP ASSISTANT

Shortly after the season, but before summer ball began the athletic department at Oakwood named their coaches who would be taking over the following Spring. The new skipper Brilie Walker was well known as a three sport star when she attended Oakwood as a student athlete. She was a centerfielder when on the Stingers team. A blond haired blue eyed recent graduate of U Maine with a degree in physical training she would become the director of sports training, and hold an office in the exercise loft. She would be available to athletes and the general public to set-up and supervise individual training programs specific to the needs of her clients. Brilie quickly became a popular resource for the entire community, along with being an assistant field hockey coach, and Varsity skipper of the Oakwood softball nine. Brilie had an easy to approach personality that created valuable loyalties among players' umpires, and parents. Makenzie Buzzell was recently married following college graduation. An attractive brunette Makenzie and her husband purchased a home in Oakwood and planned to raise their children right there in Oakwood. Along with Makenzie's nursing career Makenzie would be hired at Oakwood Academy to assist the soccer coach as JV Coach. Along with her Softball responsibilities. There was rumor that the school nurse was contemplating retirement and Makenzie had her eyes on that position. Makenzie loved the Oakwood community and considered herself a Stinger for life. Her husband seemed to buy in to his wife's train of thought in regards to Oakwood. The hunting and fishing opportunities were many, and he loved to hunt and fish.

SUMMERBALL

The newly appointed coaches were very excited to get going. They put in for a team in the summer league. RingMy Bell had returned to China once school ended, and Carrie Barry had graduated leaving the team a skeleton of the Regional final team. The coaches wanted a summer team for their own experience as much as they wanted their players to gain from the experience. Summerball was time consuming as well as full of travel with a new tournament in a new location every weekend. Ruby Bean got some time in the circle and became a lock down pitcher. When not in the circle Beanie put some time in behind the plate as the new coaches pieced their team together. Kim Johnson was the offensive star in the relaxed atmosphere of the Summer schedule. Many of the JV's from the year before got valuable playing time in a varsity level selection of games. The highlight of the summer games was an extra inning two run bomb by Kim Johnson to win a tournament in Boston Massachusetts. Brillie came to realize that being the skipper wasn't as easy as she thought it would be. The players looked to her for all the answers. As an asst. coach she thought she had all the answers, but as head skipper she learned she had to think for others, and stay one step ahead. Coaching third base was also a learning process. She found that not all the players wanted it as much as she did. Kimberly Johnson was the exception. Brilie would pay close attention to using Kimberly in every way she could think of. Starting with teaching her to slap hit. Brilie is a lefty just like Kimberly is. With Kim's speed and skill level with the bat the new coach knew if she could teach Kim to get two bounces on a slap grounder to the left side Kim would cross first base before the opponent could get the ball there. Once on first with Kim's speed she could steal second, and possibly third depending on the catcher. Brilie considered Kim to be one of her weapons. Summerball gave the JV pitcher from the year before some much needed innings in the circle, and she held up pretty well. The skipper knew the importance of quality depth, and the development of talent. Meanwhile coach Buzzell worked with the infielders and outfielders on the skills of their positions, which would be one of the coaching staffs points of emphasis in the regular season. The new coach also took the time to teach the game of softball which she believed would make the game more enjoyable and would put everyone on the same page without her prompting. She counted on her team leaders to remind the team of important points in a contest.

BRILIE'S IN GAME CRITICALS

1. When the other team scores we must score in our next opportunity on offense. Known as answering.
2. When we score get 3 quick outs, then let's go hit again. LET'S HIT
3. When we score early keep scoring every inning to build on the lead.
4. Be in the ready position on every pitch when we are in the field.
5. Take the sure out when in the field, except maybe on a play at the plate. Out's have value.
6. Picture every hit to be hit to you, and plan out what you will do with the ball when you field it.
7. Think of the successes you will have, never possible failures.
8. Be sure to celebrate in your team mates successes.
9. Always be respectful when on the diamond.
10. There are 40,000 muscles in an elephants trunk. Just saying.
11. Put the ball in play. Avoid pop-ups and strikeouts. Think down and hard
12. Advanced thinking at the plate -'s Hit it where it is pitched outside pitches go opo. Hit it where the fielders aren't playing.

THE PHILOSOPHY OF OAKWOOD SOFTBALL

POSITIVE CONVERSATION= Shut Down anyone talking negative about our team or one of your team mates. There are many different ways to say things. Find a positive way to express yourself.

I once saw a player who with a two strike pitch, fouled the next pitch off, and someone from the bench cried out way to fight off strike three. Later in the game with 3 balls on the batter the person at the plate fouled off a pitch that was over her head and the person on the bench called out way to foul off ball four. The batter thought she had done some thing great, and lined the next pitch to right field for a hit. It is the power of positive thinking. Let's tap into it.

SKILL DEVELOPMENT AT YOUR POSITION= Get to know your position so well that you are never surprised by what happens.

REPRESENT YOUR SCHOOL AND COMMUNITY WITH RESPECT AS A ROLE MODEL= Self respect, and respect for others at all times including opponents, and umpires. Make the most of your opportunity to play High School Softball. It will go by quickly.

PRIORITIES

1. Schoolwork
2. Family and Faith
3. Softball third
Play other sports, strengthen your body in the off season.
If you want a scholarship get to your grades. Be coachable

Your High School years will go fast so make sure you take full advantage of learning the importance of being a member of a community. Surprise, surprise, much to Brilie's surprise one of the catchers on one of the teams from the Boston Tournament had enrolled at Oakwood for the Fall Semester. Oakwood being a boarding school sometimes benefits from such occurrences. The girl knew of Oakwoods excellence in softball, but Oakwood also had a fine academic program. Brilie was pleasantly surprised when she heard the news. This catcher could hit as well, and would compliment the Whammer in the two hole of the line-up. The following season looked promising with the only question mark now answered. The coaches knew the community would be behind them. In fact the season could not come too soon. Hope you enjoyed the book, and GO STINGERS!!!!!!!!!!!!

WENDY PEPPERCORN ARRIVES
AT OAKWOOD FROM BOSTON

With the start of school in the fall of 2021 The Fall sports had begun. The new coach of the Oakwood Stingers Softball nine was also the Strength and Conditioning coach, so Brilie got to meet all athletes at Oakwood. It was in the weight room that Brilie first met Wendy Peppercorn. Wendy as it turned out was trying out for the Field Hockey team. This made Brilie very happy as she loved her softball players playing other sports. Brilie played Field Hockey herself when she attended Oakwood. And many of the softball players were on the Field Hockey Team, including the Whammer, and Beanie. When Ring My Bell came in from China she would join the team as well. Brilie would be very impressed by Wendy's work ethic in the weight room. Wendy was a little over 5 feet tall with stunning long black hair which she frequently wore in a pony braid. Her beautiful brown eyes caught your attention quickly. Wendy would play basketball as well as softball. With her easy going manner she made friends easily. Not just with the girls but with the boys as well. They affectionately called her Pep. It was not long into the fall season that she began dating the quarterback on the football team. The Field Hockey and Basketball team would make the playoffs but be eliminated before the Regional.

BRILIE SETS UP SPRING TRIP SOUTH

Knowing how the slow winter snow melt sets Maine teams back. The new coach wanted to take her team to Connecticut for some outdoor softball in February. The team ran raffles and made and delivered lobster rolls for super bowl Sunday to pay expenses. Once again the community showed it's support. The parents were invited and along with practice there were scrimmages set up with two high school teams. Brilie set up cribbage tournaments and a Parcheese tournament for night time activities. The Stingers, Brilie would learn, take their Parcheese very seriously. After 3 days on the practice field the Stingers were ready for their first scrimmage.

OAKWOOD WINS SCRIMMAGE IN CONNECTICUT

Ring My Bell was in the circle to start, with Wendy Peppercorn behind the plate, and JJ Johnson at second, and the Whammer in her new position centerfield. Brilie loved The Whammer in the leadoff spot with all her speed and hidden power. Wendy batted second with Beanie up third. It just sounded like runs to the coaching staff. The game moved slowly as could be expected in the early season. The pitching was well ahead of the offense. The score was 0-0 in the top of the 7th and the Whammer due up. Before Kim stepped into the box Brilie called time and motioned the Whammer over. Coach Brilie told Kim this is the time for the slapper. You've practiced it now get us a baserunner. The Whammer strode up to the plate in her usual intimidating stroll. Before the first pitch to her she reminded herself two hops to shortstop, and fly. The pitch was on the outside corner, perfect for a slap hit. On contact Whammer was already on her way to first. As Brilie saw the second hop she felt all warm and fuzzy inside. When she looked up Kim was already past first, man she thought that girl can fly. The shortstop made a clean play on the ball and a good throw, there was just no chance of getting the ball to first ahead of Kim. As Whammer returned to the bag she and Brilie were both smiling as they pointed at one another in joy. As Whammer looked over Brilie was walking backwards away from Kim which was the steal sign. Why wait Brilie thought we got speed to burn. Let's use it. Wendy Peppercorn was the next hitter and Brilie was careful not to walk towards her because that would be the bunt sign. Coach did not want a bunt here ;she wanted a swipe then a hit. Whammer was off on the first pitch, and dove head first safely into second. The cheering section screamed and applauded

Whammer's effort. Brilie yelled out "Nice swipe way to go kid." Wendy would work the count to 3-0 before hitting a ball off the wall in left field scoring the winning run as it would turn out as RingMy would shut down the opponent in the bottom of the 7th. She would finish with 19 strikeouts, 0 walks, 3 hits, and 0 runs. The winner of the game ball was Whammer for her offense but she made two catches in the outfield, both catches were on the run. The team joined their opponent for a cookout. The next time they would be in Summerball. The coaches considered the spring training practice and game a win. Now it was home and get ready for the start of league play.

FIRST GAME OF 2021

The first game of the new season would be scheduled as a road game at Pine Tree Academy. Their field was covered with snow and thus unplayable. The Athletic Directors therefore decided to flip home games to stay on schedule. Oakwood would therefore travel to Pine Tree later in the season. Kudos to the maintenance crew for their work on the Oakwood field. Brilie and the team were glad to be starting the season on time, because they were ready.

The Pine Tree pitcher,now a Senior, was the same pitcher that pitched against Oakwood the year before in the Regional at ST. JOE'S. RING My was fresh off a summer where she pitched for the China Olympic Team. The score was 0-0 through 5 innings when the top of the Oakwood batting order came up for their second look at the Pine Tree pitcher. Leading off was The Whammer. Kim took 4 pitches, and with the count 3-1,the Pine Tree pitcher left a pitch up in the strike zone and Kim did not miss it. She roped a topspin drive into right field that dove to the ground in front of the right fielder. With Whammer on first Brilie began walking backward in the third base coaches box. Kim was expecting it, as was Wendy now in the right handed batters box. On the next pitch Kim was off, diving into second base safely. All of this seemed to unnerve the Pine Tree pitcher. The Stingers had seen this in the Regional the year before where this pitcher had lost her strike zone. Wendy walked on 4 pitches. With runners now on first and second and no outs Beanie strode to the plate. Beanies long blond pony braid trailing her as she went. Beanie was a beautiful high school Senior with blue eyes, and a very athletic body. The Oakwood faithful cheered as Beanie's name was announced. After working the count in her favor 3-1 Beanie lifted a fastball up high and far, and into the Oakwood fans beyond the left field barrier for a home run. The three girls circled the bases, and were met by the rest of the Oakwood team at home plate, where they all celebrated Beanie's blast.

Pine Tree would answer in the top of the seventh with back to back doubles and a base hit. The result was two runs scored. The Stingers would leave the field with a 3-2 victory over a very good team. Their next game would be the following Tuesday at home against Maplewood. Brilie and Makenzie could not be happier. They could see how the trip south put them ahead of other Maine teams. The goals were first to make the playoffs, then to have a home playoff game, if they could accomplish that they would set new goals at that time.

BUILDING TEAM UNITY
Each player was given a sheet of paper that had everyone's name on it. The coach would write every comment on one sheet of paper and give each player a copy of all the comments. Players came to know what their team mates liked about them. From I like how you smell, to I like how fearless you are. Some of the players carried their list everywhere they went.

PHOTOS

Printed in the United States
by Baker & Taylor Publisher Services